MENANDWOMEN
WWW.MOSAIXSTUDY.COM

# MENANDWOMEN
## www.mosaixstudy.com

### toben & joanne heim

NAVPRESS

Bringing Truth to Life
P.O. Box 35001, Colorado Springs, Colorado 80935

**OUR GUARANTEE TO YOU**

We believe so strongly in the message of our books that we are making this quality guarantee to you. If for any reason you are disappointed with the content of this book, return the title page to us with your name and address and we will refund to you the list price of the book. To help us serve you better, please briefly describe why you were disappointed. Mail your refund request to: NavPress, P.O. Box 35002, Colorado Springs, CO 80935.

The Navigators is an international Christian organization. Our mission is to reach, disciple, and equip people to know Christ and to make Him known through successive generations. We envision multitudes of diverse people in the United States and every other nation who have a passionate love for Christ, live a lifestyle of sharing Christ's love, and multiply spiritual laborers among those without Christ.

NavPress is the publishing ministry of The Navigators. NavPress publications help believers learn biblical truth and apply what they learn to their lives and ministries. Our mission is to stimulate spiritual formation among our readers.

© 2001 by The Navigators
All rights reserved. No part of this publication may be reproduced in any form without written permission from NavPress, P.O. Box 35001, Colorado Springs, CO 80935.
www.navpress.com
Library of Congress Catalog Card Number: 2001031233
ISBN 1-57683-268-6

Cover design by Ray Moore
Cover digital illustration by Paul Price/Digital Vision
Creative Team: Paul Santhouse, Karen Lee-Thorp, Darla Hightower, Ray Moore, Pat Miller

Some of the anecdotal illustrations in this book are true to life and are included with the permission of the persons involved. All other illustrations are composites of real situations, and any resemblance to people living or dead is coincidental.

Unless otherwise identified, all Scripture quotations in this publication are taken from *The Message: New Testament with Psalms and Proverbs* by Eugene H. Peterson, copyright © 1993, 1994, 1995, used by permission of NavPress Publishing Group. Other versions used include: the HOLY BIBLE: NEW INTERNATIONAL VERSION® (NIV®). Copyright © 1973, 1978, 1984 by International Bible Society. Used by permission of Zondervan Publishing House. All rights reserved.

Heim, Toben, 1970-
   Mosaixstudy.com/menandwomen / Toben & Joanne Heim.
   p.cm.
   ISBN 1-57683-268-6
   1. Friendship—Religious aspects—Christianity. 2. Man-woman relationships—Religious aspects—Christianity. I. Title: Mosaixstudy dot com slash men and women. II. Heim, Joanne, 1972- III. Title.
BV4647.F7 H45 2001
248.8'4—dc21

2001031233

---

FOR A FREE CATALOG OF
NAVPRESS BOOKS & BIBLE STUDIES,
CALL 1-800-366-7788 (USA)
OR 1-416-499-4615 (CANADA)

---

Printed in the United States of America

1 2 3 4 5 6 7 8 9 10 / 05 04 03 02 01

# CONTENTS

- How This Study Works. . . . . . . . . . . . . . . . . . . . . . . . . 7
- Doing This Study with a Group. . . . . . . . . . . . . . . . . . 10

**BIG IDEA #1**
- If It's Not Romance, How Does It Work?. . . . . . . . . . . . . . . 12

**BIG IDEA #2**
- What Are My Boundaries?. . . . . . . . . . . . . . . . . . . . . . 24

**BIG IDEA #3**
- How Can I Be a Safe Person?. . . . . . . . . . . . . . . . . . . . 38

**BIG IDEA #4**
- What Are My Motives?. . . . . . . . . . . . . . . . . . . . . . . . 50

**BIG IDEA #5**
- How Important Are Gender Differences?. . . . . . . . . . . . . . 62

- Wrapping It Up: So What?. . . . . . . . . . . . . . . . . . . . . . 70
- Notes. . . . . . . . . . . . . . . . . . . . . . . . . . . . . . . . . 76

## mosaixstudy.com/menandwomen—
# HOW THIS STUDY WORKS

**I**F you're married or dating, chances are that you spend a fair amount of time thinking, talking, and searching the Bible for answers about how you should relate to the opposite sex in that kind of relationship. If you have children, maybe you read parenting books or talk with other parents about the joys and challenges of a parent-child relationship.

But what about your *other* relationships with people of the opposite sex? How much time do you spend thinking, talking, or reading about how you relate to ministry partners, coworkers, and friends? We've asked dozens of people this question, and we learned three things:

1. Everybody has opposite-sex relationships at various degrees of intimacy, from strictly business to close friends.
2. Almost nobody spends much time thinking about how to relate to those people in God-honoring ways.
3. When they stop to think about it, almost everybody admits to having real struggles in those relationships.

This study is designed to address those struggles. Together we'll examine our own experiences, the experiences of others, and the Bible as we ask how men and women can be friends and colleagues. How can we get the most out of those relationships wisely, in a way that honors God and others?

The study is divided into six chapters—five big ideas and a last chapter that will help you answer the question "So what?" Each of these big ideas about men and women is divided into smaller sections and has a number of different elements. The smaller sections can stand alone, so you can do some of them or all of them, or mix them up in a different order. The various elements are designed to appeal to different styles of thinking and learning—you can select the ones that work for you and leave the rest.

## mosaixstudy.com/menandwomen—
## HOW THIS STUDY WORKS (CONT'D)

- *Text about friendships between men and women.* This text is designed to share information, background, or specific teaching about the topic.

- *Bible passages.* Most Bible passages come from *The Message*. We like using *The Message* because if you're familiar with the Bible, *The Message* gives a new twist on a passage you may have read a million times before. Sometimes hearing something put a new way can transform your perspective. Also, if you're new to the Bible, *The Message* says things in everyday language that doesn't require expertise to understand. Feel free to look at other Bible versions too.

- *Short essays.* One of the fun things about getting to know other people is hearing their stories. These essays give a glimpse into how someone else has experienced relationships with the opposite sex.

- *Questions.* You'll find questions about your experience, about a Bible passage, and about your general ideas or opinions.

- *Activities.* Not everyone learns in the same way. That's why we included ideas for drawing, performing, building things—all kinds of hands-on ways to grapple with the issue of men and women.

- *Quotes from "experts."* We've quoted a number of "experts" throughout this study to give you an idea of what more experienced and knowledgeable people have written, thought, or said about this topic.

8

# HOW THIS STUDY WORKS (CONT'D)

mosaixstudy.com/menandwomen—

- *Quotes from ordinary people.* We also asked ordinary people what they thought about some of the ideas in this study. They vary in age and background, and come from different parts of the country (even the world!). Some are believers; some are not.

- *Resource information.* This isn't the definitive work on men and women. We've included these resources as additional ways to learn more about this topic.

# mosaixstudy.com/menandwomen—
# DOING THIS STUDY AS A GROUP

IF you want to use this study with a group, here are a few ideas that should help make that a fun and productive experience.

- First, it might be a good idea to find a facilitator. Maybe that's you.

- Find a few friends (or potential friends) to work through the book together. Your enthusiasm will get everyone else excited about it too.

- Set a time (weekly, biweekly, monthly) to get everyone together. It works best to set a regular time to meet and get it scheduled in advance. Everyone is so busy that if you don't set up regular times to meet, it may be difficult or impossible to get everyone together.

- Set some ground rules as a group. Talk about things like purpose (why are you getting together?), participation (what does it mean to be part of the group?), attendance (how important is it for everyone to be there each time you meet?), confidentiality (will what's said in the group stay in the group?), and accessibility (how open is everyone to being available to the other members of the group?).

- Agree about how much preparation people will do before each meeting. Ideally, you'll cover one big idea per meeting. For each big idea, you could select sections and exercises ahead of time for group members to prepare. It's not necessary (or even possible!) to cover all the questions and exercises during group time. You may find that some people will want to do the hands-on projects and bring them to the group to share, and others will dig into the verbal questions and want to talk about those. This diversity is not a problem as long as you focus your group time on the big idea. It's wise to have everybody come prepared to talk about one or two of the Bible passages (you can pick which ones ahead of time) and to share anything else that hit them as important in the study.

- Encourage group members to get together between regular meetings, send e-mail, or make occasional phone calls to each other. This will continue to build those friendships that will make your times together more fun and more comfortable for everyone.

## mosaixstudy.com/menandwomen—
## DOING THIS STUDY AS A GROUP (CONT'D)

- If you sense that someone really isn't into the group or is losing interest, take the time to ask him or her what's up. The reason for the disconnect may be something easy to fix.

- Different people in your group are going to have different communication styles and comfort levels when it comes to sharing their stories. Be sensitive to these differences. You may have to do a little extra work to draw out the quiet people or to make sure the more vocal members of the group don't bury them.

After things get going, feel free to let others try their hand at facilitation. That will increase their ownership in the group and will give you a chance to sit back and participate without the responsibility for keeping things moving.

Regardless of how you decide to structure your time together, keep in mind that it may be difficult to get as much done as you'd hoped with each meeting. If it takes you twice as long to get through a section as you thought it would, that's probably a good thing. It means everyone is really getting into it!

# WHEN HARRY MET SALLY

Once there was a guy named Harry who met a girl named Sally. They became friends—or what she called friends. Harry called it something different—and that changed depending on when you asked him.

If you haven't seen the 1989 film *When Harry Met Sally*, rent it. Just about every conversation about friendship between men and women these days seems to begin with a discussion of this movie.

> No man can be friends with a woman he finds attractive. He always wants to have sex with her. Sex is always out there. Friendship is ultimately doomed and that is the end of the story.
> —HARRY TO SALLY, *WHEN HARRY MET SALLY* [1]

## 12 — If it's not ROMANCE how does it work?

**ONE BIG IDEA**

Do you agree with Harry's statement above? Why, or why not?

What role does attraction play in male-female relationships?

If Harry's statement is true, does that mean there's no problem with being friends with someone you're *not* attracted to?

**DO** Rent *When Harry Met Sally* and set aside some time to watch it together as a group—maybe a Friday night apart from your usual meeting time. Pop some popcorn, watch the movie, and prepare for a big discussion afterward!

MENANDWOMEN
www.mosaixstudy.com

# BIG IDEA ONE

**CAN MEN AND WOMEN BE FRIENDS?** Most classical thinkers thought friendship between men and women was impossible. Maybe that's because men and women led such separate lives in classical times—women weren't educated or involved in politics or public life, and many men spent huge quantities of time away from home fighting wars. But while times have changed and the gap in experiences between men and women has shrunk, not everyone agrees that men and women can be friends.

*Yes, yes, yes! I have had great relationships with men as friends. The trick is to lay the groundwork early. Have the discussion about what your expectations are of the friendship and don't change the rules halfway through the relationship.*

—SARAH

*Sometimes. There can be complications when both people are single. One of them usually becomes more involved than the other and then the friendship either becomes a romantic relationship or they are no longer friends.*

—ANGELA

*Absolutely! Many of my best friendships are with men. For the most part, my friendships with men last longer and are healthier than several of my friendships with women. They are able to give me a perspective that I can't get from my girlfriends. I find that guys hold fewer grudges, are less likely to ask if they look fat, and will shoot straight with me. I don't have to keep my radar for problems turned up as high as I do with women friends.*

—LISA

*I should hope men and women can be friends—God designed them to be. However, men and women are wired differently and this can complicate friendships—but it doesn't have to. It just means you have to be aware of the differences and make allowances. I think these differences enhance friendships, not hinder them.*

—GLENN

*No. I don't think men and women can be friends. I've seen too many couples get divorced because the husband or wife was friends with someone of the opposite sex and they ended up getting involved. Those are never the people that they intended to have an affair with, but I've seen it happen too many times to be comfortable with it.*

—STEVE

*If it's not* **ROMANCE** *how does it work?*

# If it's not ROMANCE how does it work?

## 14

## ONE BIG IDEA

What do you think? Can men and women be friends? Why, or why not?

> A woman may very well form a friendship with a man, but for this to endure, it must be assisted by a little physical antipathy.
> —**Friedrich Nietzsche**[2]

> I have always laid it down as a maxim—and found it justified by experience—that a man and a woman make far better friendships than can exist between two of the same sex—but *then* with the condition that they never have made or are to make love to each other.
> —**Lord Byron**[3]

> Economic, political, psychological, and other differences between the genders result in the fact that women find it difficult to be friends with men and vice versa.
> —**Mary Hunt**, *Fierce Tenderness: A Feminist Theology of Friendship*[4]
>
> Between men and women there is no friendship possible. There is passion, enmity, worship, love, but no friendship.
> —**Oscar Wilde**[5]
>
> Friendship can only exist between persons with similar interests and points of view. Man and woman by the conventions of society are born with different interests and different points of view.
> —**J. August Strindberg**, *The Son of a Servant*[6]
>
> Friendship between men and women will always have to face certain difficulties that will not be present in same-sex friendships.
> —**Gilbert Meilaender**, "Men and Women—Can We Be Friends?"[7]

MENANDWOMEN
www.mosaixstudy.com

## BIG IDEA ONE

## If it's not ROMANCE how does it work?

**WHAT DO YOU MEAN BY "FRIENDS"?** Your views on male-female friendships are probably influenced by how you define "friend." Instead of asking whether men and women can be friends, it might be more helpful to ask:

- How close a non-romantic friendship can you have with someone of the opposite sex?

- What qualities do you seek in an opposite-sex friend?

> People today, especially younger people, are much likelier to have opposite-sex friendships than were their parents. Friendships are equal-status relationships, and the sexes have unquestionably become more equal in all areas. Women and men now work in many of the same offices, at the same careers, providing considerably more opportunity for them to get to know one another on a casual basis.
>
> —LINDA SAPADIN, PH.D.[8]

*Before I became a believer in my freshman year of college, my life pretty much reflected Harry's statement. I had some level of sexual contact with most of my female friends. It was, it seemed, inevitable that relational intimacy would lead to sexual intimacy given enough time and opportunity.*

*But I think one of the beautiful things about the redemption we experience in Christ is the opportunity to resist this sort of fatalistic thinking when it comes to men and women in friendship with one another.*

*Since then, I've had probably a dozen close female friends, none of which have led to sex, and all of which have led to a richer life. It's difficult for me to imagine what my life would be like without the life-giving presence of my close female friends.*

—ADAM

# 16
## If it's not ROMANCE how does it work?

**ONE BIG IDEA**

○ List or circle five to ten qualities or characteristics you seek in a friend or a friendship.

> Confidence
> Trust
> Trustworthiness
> Commitment
> Communication
> Listening
> Honesty
> Community
> Ability to accept/give constructive criticism
> Shared interests
> Shared values
> Fun
> Sense of humor
> Athletic skill
> Growth
> Intentionality
> Emotional stability
> Financial stability
> Availability

Are those qualities different for an opposite-sex friendship as opposed to a same-sex one? If so, how? If not, why not?

List five to ten qualities or characteristics you seek in a marriage or romantic partner. Exclude "sex" and "raising children together."

MENANDWOMEN
WWW.MOSAIXSTUDY.COM

## BIG IDEA ONE

In what ways are the qualities you want in a friend like those you want in a romantic partner? In what ways are they different?

For most of us, there is overlap in qualities we are looking for in a friend and in a romantic partner. That may be why these friendships seem ambiguous. With the exception of one or two things, we could easily find ourselves romantically linked to this other person. And that's why boundaries and communication are so critical to keeping these friendships healthy. We'll cover boundaries and communication in more detail in Big Idea #2.

> Not very long ago, a heterosexual man and woman had only one kind of relationship—a romantic one. But fortunately, that's changing.
> —**Russell Wild, "The Friendship Challenge"** [9]

**DO** Spend some time thinking about friendship. How would you communicate what a friend is to the rest of the group? Make a collage, draw a picture, or write a poem to share.

17

*If it's not* **ROMANCE** *how does it work?*

**HOW DOES THE BIBLE DEFINE FRIENDSHIP?** For each of the following passages, come up with a word or phrase that describes the quality or characteristic of biblical friendship the passage reflects. Then discuss whether or not that quality can apply to male-female friendships or to single-gender friendships only. Take a couple of minutes to see if you can find other applicable verses and do the same exercise with them.

*If it's not* **ROMANCE** *how does it work?*

# ONE BIG IDEA

> You use steel to sharpen steel, and one friend sharpens another. (Proverbs 27:17)
>
> "Be alert. If you see your friend going wrong, correct him. If he responds, forgive him." (Luke 17:3)
>
> "This is the very best way to love. Put your life on the line for your friends." (John 15:13)
>
> Be good friends who love deeply; practice playing second fiddle. (Romans 12:10)
>
> Laugh with your happy friends when they're happy; share tears when they're down. Get along with each other; don't be stuck-up. Make friends with nobodies; don't be the great somebody. (Romans 12:15-16)
>
> For instance, you come upon an old friend dressed in rags and half-starved and say, "Good morning, friend! Be clothed in Christ! Be filled with the Holy Spirit!" and walk off without providing so much as a coat or a cup of soup—where does that get you? (James 2:15-16)

MENANDWOMEN
www.mosaixstudy.com

# BIG IDEA ONE

# 19

## If it's not ROMANCE how does it work?

**"THAT'S NOT WHAT I MEANT!"** Most of us would be uncomfortable expressing ourselves so freely that what we say might be "difficult on occasion to distinguish from sexual harassment." And if the hearer happens to be a friend you work with, having your words mistaken as sexual harassment could get you sued or fired ... or both. If you are friends in another environment, those words could cost you a friendship.

> Friendship requires an easy spontaneity, a willingness to say what one thinks, talk with few holds barred and few matters off limits—precisely the sort of thing that some will find difficult on occasion to distinguish from sexual harassment.
>
> —GILBERT MEILAENDER, "MEN AND WOMEN—CAN WE BE FRIENDS?"[10]

When we read a quote like the one from Gilbert Meilaender above, we tend to assume that the man is the offender and the woman is the offended. Is that usually the case? Why, or why not?

**DO** The great debate: If you are in a mixed-gender group, divide into two teams: men and women. Men, start first and address the Meilaender quote above. Do you buy Meilaender's assertion? Are there limits to what you communicate? How can you be entirely honest without getting into trouble—or can you be? While the men are talking, the women should listen closely without commenting.
After ten minutes, switch. Women, start by summing up, in a minute or less, what you heard the men say. Then respond. Do you agree or disagree with what the men among you have said? How does the female perspective differ from the male one? When the women have completed their comments, men, take a minute to sum up what you've heard. If you think the women misunderstood you, this is the time to clarify. Spend some time making sure that everyone understands what the others have said, even if you disagree. Finally, discuss how your views or behaviors might change based on what you've heard. What surprised you?

Do you think your marital status affects your friendships with the opposite sex? If so, how? If not, why?

## 20 — If it's not ROMANCE how does it work?

*It's like my "internal dialog" gets switched off and the words just come out. Mostly it happens when I'm trying to be funny or when I'm agitated about something. Sometimes what comes out isn't really appropriate for mixed company. One time a female friend actually slapped me for making a not-too-nice comment about a female police officer who gave me a speeding ticket.*
—BRANDON

## ONE BIG IDEA

If you're married, what role does your spouse play in your friendships with the opposite sex? If you're single, how do you think your friendships with the opposite sex might change were you to marry?

*Don't expect your friendships to be the same when one friend gets married.*
—LISA

**DO** — Many of our assumptions about male-female friendships come from the media. Spend some time collecting images, video clips, quotes from books, or any other sources that have influenced your assumptions about these relationships. Share what you find with the group.

MENANDWOMEN
WWW.MOSAIXSTUDY.COM

## WHO'S IN YOUR LIFE?

Do you have opposite-sex friends? If so, write a list of their names.

There are probably also plenty of opposite-sex people in your life whom you don't define as your own "friends." These include coworkers, friends of your spouse or partner, relatives of your spouse, and so on. List six to ten of these people.

**DO** It's time to take a quick look at the differences between those relationships you defined as friends and those in the second group—let's call those "others." Take a piece of paper and on one side, write down some characteristics for your friends group. How do those relationships work? On the other side, write down characteristics of your relationships with the "others" group. Focus most of your attention on your attitudes, behaviors, and thoughts related to these two distinct groups. Your list might include words like warm, sterile, trusting, affectionate, businesslike, no-nonsense, fun, and so on. Discuss with your group the essence of what makes those relationships distinct and why.

*If it's not* **ROMANCE** *how does it work?*

## 22 — If it's not ROMANCE how does it work?

Lovers are normally face to face, absorbed in each other; Friends, side by side, absorbed in some common interest.

—C. S. Lewis[11]

To the query, "What is a friend?" his reply was "A single soul dwelling in two bodies."

—Aristotle[12]

[In friendship] we are being prepared ultimately for that vast friendship which is heaven, in which we truly are taken beyond ourselves, and in which all share the love of God.

—Gilbert Meilaender,
"Men and Women—Can We Be Friends?"[13]

## BIG IDEA ONE

> When I see a single man and woman develop a friendship, I immediately assume it is because one or the other desires something more than friendship. When I was single, the pressure was on to find a man! If a guy wanted to be my friend, I accepted based on whether or not I could see future mate potential in him.
>
> —Megan

**DO** Grab a concordance or Bible software and look up *friend*, *friends*, and *friendship*. On a big piece of paper, list the verse references you find. You'll be amazed how long the list is. If you have more time, write down what the Bible has to say in each instance.

### AS A GROUP—OR ON YOUR OWN

Your answer to the question of men and women being friends largely depends on your definition of friendship. Examining your thoughts and attitudes about friendship helps give clarity when talking about male-female friendships.

MENANDWOMEN
www.mosaixstudy.com

# BIG IDEA ONE

## AS A GROUP—OR ON YOUR OWN (cont'd)

How has this discussion changed your thoughts about the people in your life? Do you consider some people "friends" that you hadn't before thought of as friends? Are some of the people you thought were "friends" not really friends as you define them?

What questions do you still have about male-female friendships? Keep these in mind as you continue this study. If you're doing this study with a group, you may want to ask the other members for their input on your questions.

If you're doing this study as a group, how has this discussion affected how you view your group? For example, if your group is mixed, do you view the members of the opposite sex differently than you did when the discussion began? If so, how?

*If it's not* **ROMANCE** *how does it work?*

23

## THE LAW VS. BOUNDARIES

Because of the potential hazards in male-female relationships, it's tempting to come up with a list of rules and regulations to slap on everyone.

At the same time, because we're all individuals in unique situations, it's hard to find rules that fit everyone equally well. So how do we determine what's right for us, for the other person, and for both of us as we interact together?

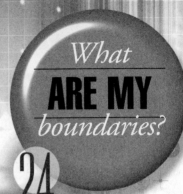

*What* **ARE MY** *boundaries?*

24

**BIG IDEA TWO**

The key is boundaries. Boundaries define who we are; they draw the line between what is me and what is not me. In *Boundaries*, Dr. Cloud and Dr. Townsend write, "Boundaries are anything that helps to differentiate you from someone else, or shows where you begin and end."[1] Here are a few examples of boundaries:

**If you're** interested in learning more about boundaries, pick up a copy of *Boundaries* by Dr. Henry Cloud and Dr. John Townsend (Zondervan). A companion workbook is also available.

- Skin. Our skin shows where we begin and end. Physically, we are separate from others.

- Words. Our words define who we are as we communicate thoughts, feelings, intentions, and so on. Words let others know where we stand in relation to them.

MENANDWOMEN
WWW.MOSAIXSTUDY.COM

- Reality. God is real. God is who God is, not just what we imagine him to be. God has created a real world that is what it is, no matter what fantasy worlds we may imagine. Being honest about who we are and what is real helps us set boundaries that deal with the real world.

- Geographical distance. It's sometimes appropriate to put distance between us and another person when that person is dangerous or when the relationship has become inappropriate.

- Time. Taking time off from someone else can be an effective way to untangle ourselves from that person.

- Emotional distance. This temporary boundary gives us a chance to heal emotionally and separate ourselves from hurt until we are ready to trust again.

- Other people. Other people can help us set and maintain boundaries. Support from others is invaluable when creating boundaries.

- Consequences. Consequences are a natural part of life, and we need to back up our boundaries with consequences. Consequences let others know we mean business and show the seriousness of violating our boundaries.

*What* **ARE MY** *boundaries?*

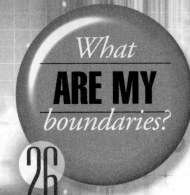

## What ARE MY boundaries? 26

What's within our boundaries? The defining characteristic is responsibility. We can only control our own behavior. So what are the things that each of us is responsible for as we relate to other people?

- Feelings. Our feelings are our responsibility. Other people are not responsible for how we feel. If there's a problem, we need to address it.

- Attitudes and beliefs. Even though most of our attitudes and beliefs were formed at an early age, we are still responsible for how we think about things.

- Behaviors. We are responsible for the consequences of our own actions. We are not responsible for the consequences of others' actions, and they are not responsible for ours.

- Choices. No one can make us do anything. We are responsible for our choices—even if it doesn't feel like it.

- Values. What we love affects the choices we make. We are responsible for what we hold dear.

- Limits. We can't set limits on others, but we can limit our exposure to them.

- Thoughts. We are responsible for our internal monologue.

- Desires. We are responsible for what we want and how we go about getting those things.

- Love. We are responsible for how we give and receive love.

It's easy to confuse boundaries with legalism. Sometimes when we set boundaries, others respond by accusing us of being legalistic. But legalism is primarily the belief that we can earn God's favor (or someone else's) by checking things off a list. Legalism is inflexible, often seeks to control others, and is more concerned with outward conformity than inward maturity.

> Christians should not barely consider what was in itself lawful to be done, but what was fit for them to do.
> —**Matthew Henry**[2]

**TWO BIG IDEA**

MENANDWOMEN
www.mosaixstudy.com

# BIG IDEA TWO

By contrast, boundaries aren't set in stone. Part of the process of setting healthy boundaries is evaluating how well they're working and readjusting if necessary. Boundaries are concerned with our own behavior and choices, not with controlling others. Boundaries are never manipulative tools to make the other person give us love or friendship.

Take a good look at the list of things we're each responsible for—those things within our boundaries. Have you given responsibility for any of those things to other people? (For example, have you given a member of the opposite sex responsibility for your feelings—perhaps blaming the person for not feeling the same way?)

Think about your desires as they relate to your opposite-sex friendships. Have you taken responsibility for what you want those friendships to be like? Or have you instead bemoaned that things aren't the way you'd like? What steps can you take to make those friendships the way you'd like them to be?

> *I think boundaries have more to do with what I will or won't do based on who I know myself to be. Rules don't care about who I am or what situation I'm in.*
> —DAVID

> *I don't think I have many boundaries. I'm a really open person and I pretty much just let it hang out there. A couple times I've gotten in trouble because I trusted someone I shouldn't have or have been more self-disclosing than was appropriate, so now I try to be a little more careful. But my tendency is still to just be myself.*
> —DONNA

Pick one other item from the list on p. 26 and think about how it relates to your opposite-sex friendships. How can you take responsibility for that area of your life? What do you think the result might be if you did?

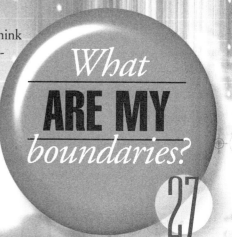

What ARE MY *boundaries?*

## What are my boundaries? 28

**WHAT'S APPROPRIATE FOR ME?** It's rarely good enough for us to ask questions about our thoughts or behaviors in terms of black or white. More often we deal in a grayer realm, asking questions about who we are and what's appropriate in the situations in which we find ourselves. Maybe it's in our nature to rebel against rules, but it's in our best interest to have a firm grasp on what's appropriate based on who and where we are.

Can you tell the group about a time when you did something in a relationship that wasn't really wrong, but probably wasn't appropriate considering the situation?

## TWO BIG IDEA

What factors might a person consider in deciding if or how they should be friends with someone of the opposite sex? If you feel comfortable doing so, share some things with the group that you know about yourself that shape your decision-making process about these relationships.

> To learn to see beyond our own secret countries — to what is at the same time both terrible and beautiful — is, from the perspective of Christian faith, the purpose of friendship. And to the degree that friendship not only with those of our own sex but with those of the opposite sex may more fully enable such a vision, we have every reason to attempt it, despite its inherent difficulties.
>
> —GILBERT MEILAENDER, "MEN AND WOMEN—CAN WE BE FRIENDS?"³

MENANDWOMEN
WWW.MOSAIXSTUDY.COM

# BIG IDEA TWO

> I had a really close woman friend at my office. She was actually my boss. She was single and a little older than me but we liked the same bands and so we went out a lot to concerts and stuff. I heard from one of the other guys I work with that she told someone she liked me. I pretty much freaked out because even though nothing had happened, this was a person who could fire me. I had to think back about the time we had spent together to see if I sent her any signals or said anything that I should be worried about. In the end I told her that I didn't think we should hang out anymore. I wanted to put an end to it before anything got out of control. Maybe we can hang out again sometime but for now I think it's best for both of us to just take some time off.
>
> —JEREMY

In 1 Corinthians Paul talks a lot about what is appropriate and what isn't. Twice in chapter 6 and twice again in chapter 10 Paul says, "Everything is permissible for me but not everything is beneficial" (NIV). Paul had taught the Corinthians about freedom in Christ, but apparently a few of them had misinterpreted him and used that teaching as a license to do whatever they wanted. See how Paul worked to correct their faulty thinking in the passages below:

> Just because something is technically legal doesn't mean that it's spiritually appropriate. If I went around doing whatever I thought I could get by with, I'd be a slave to my whims. (1 Corinthians 6:12)

> Looking at it one way, you could say, "Anything goes. Because of God's immense generosity and grace, we don't have to dissect and scrutinize every action to see if it will pass muster." But the point is not to just get by. (1 Corinthians 10:23)

Paul is talking about two different things in these passages. In the first he's talking about sexual immorality. In the second he's talking about eating meat that's been sacrificed to idols. But beyond that, he is talking about doing what is appropriate, considering who we are and in what situation we find ourselves. Technically legal isn't good enough.

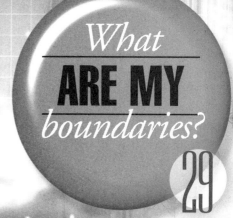

*What* **ARE MY** *boundaries?*

## What ARE MY boundaries?

**30**

**?** What would "just getting by" look like in the context of a male-female friendship?

**TWO BIG IDEA**

What do you know to be true of yourself as it relates to friendships with the opposite sex? How have you discovered these things about yourself? How do you draw on this knowledge in making decisions about your opposite-sex relationships?

**DO** This is a big exercise but well worth it. Read 1 Corinthians 6–10. In these chapters Paul talks at length about making good, ethical decisions in our relationships. As you read the chapters, make a list of "decision-making principles" that you could apply to your opposite-sex relationships. As you discover these principles, see if you can arrange the few that seem most applicable into a series of questions that you would ask yourself when faced with an uncertain relational situation. Share your discoveries with the group.

MENANDWOMEN
www.mosaixstudy.com

# BIG IDEA TWO

**LET'S PLAY "WHAT IF?"** If you did the exercise, on page 30 on 1 Corinthians 6–10, use the questions you came up with to work through the following scenarios. If you haven't read 1 Corinthians, you can take a run at these scenarios anyway.

- You are a man with a woman friend. You have been friends for some time, but during the course of your relationship you fall in love with someone else. The person you fall in love with is uncomfortable with the nature of this other relationship. What do you do?

- You are a married woman involved in a ministry at your church with a handful of other men and women. One night after a team meeting you need a ride home. One of the guys in the group volunteers. You accept the ride—after all, this guy is a friend. When the ministry team meets the next week, someone else on the team approaches you to say she was uncomfortable with the fact that you and this guy left together. After all, one of you is married. What do you say?

- You are close friends with a person of the opposite sex—you've been friends for years. You marry someone else. After you're married (because you're paying a little more attention), you realize that your spouse is uncomfortable with that friendship. What do you do?

> *I can usually tell if a friendship isn't "just a friendship" to that other person—meaning, if they are flirting with me or something. If there is inappropriate behavior or conversation taking place, then I know it isn't an appropriate relationship.*
>
> **—JENNIFER**

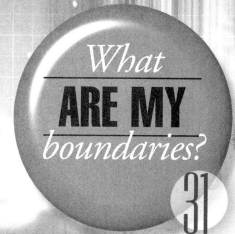

*What* **ARE MY** *boundaries?*

**SHOWING DEFERENCE** What is deference? It means "courteous submission to the opinion, wishes, or judgment of another; courteous respect."[4]

In 1 Corinthians 6–10, Paul discusses deference several times, most notably in chapters 8 and 10. Here's what he has to say:

*What* **ARE MY** *boundaries?*

32

> But God *does* care when you use your freedom carelessly in a way that leads a Christian still vulnerable to those old associations to be thrown off track.
>
> For instance, say you flaunt your freedom by going to a banquet thrown in honor of idols, where the main course is meat sacrificed to idols. Isn't there great danger if someone still struggling over this issue, someone who looks up to you as knowledgeable and mature, sees you go into that banquet? The danger is that he will become terribly confused—maybe even to the point of getting mixed up himself in what his conscience tells him is wrong.
>
> Christ gave up his life for that person. Wouldn't you at least be willing to give up going to dinner for him—because, as you say, it doesn't really make any difference? But it *does* make a difference if you hurt your friend terribly, risking his eternal ruin! When you hurt your friend, you hurt Christ. A free meal here and there isn't worth it at the cost of even one of these "weak ones." So, never go to these idol-tainted meals if there's any chance it will trip up one of your brothers or sisters. (1 Corinthians 8:9-13)

TWO BIG IDEA

MENANDWOMEN
www.mosaixstudy.com

# BIG IDEA TWO

> We want to live well, but our foremost efforts should be to help *others* live well....
> I'm not going to walk around on eggshells worrying about what small-minded people might say; I'm going to stride free and easy, knowing what our large-minded Master has already said. If I eat what is served to me, grateful to God for what is on the table, how can I worry about what someone will say? I thanked God for it and he blessed it!
> So eat your meals heartily, not worrying about what others say about you—you're eating to God's glory, after all, not to please them. As a matter of fact, do everything that way, heartily and freely to God's glory. At the same time, don't be callous in your exercise of freedom, thoughtlessly stepping on the toes of those who aren't as free as you are. I try my best to be considerate of everyone's feelings in all these matters; I hope you will be, too. (1 Corinthians 10:24,29-33)

What differences (if any) do you find between these two passages? What ideas do you find in common?

In 1 Corinthians 10, what's the difference between "not . . . worrying about what small-minded people might say" and "thoughtlessly stepping on the toes of those who aren't as free as you are"?

*What* **ARE MY** *boundaries?*

Paul is talking about deferring not just to our opposite-sex friends, but also to those who are looking on. His basic question to us is this: To what extent and under what circumstances do I adjust my behavior in deference to the feelings and limitations of bystanders?

Basically, Paul shows deference to people who would be genuinely led into immoral behavior themselves by his example because they aren't capable of handling the freedom that he's mature enough to handle. He doesn't show deference to those who are just "small-minded" or judgmental.

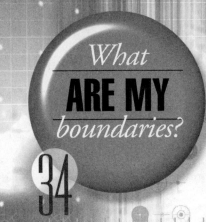

## What ARE MY boundaries?

### 34

**BIG IDEA TWO**

What's the difference between the "small-minded" and those who might genuinely be led astray by your behavior? Can you think of an example that relates to opposite-sex friendships?

Do you tend to be concerned about what others think? Is that because you don't want to lead them into sin or because you want them to like you?

When have you dealt with criticism from the small-minded? When have you misled someone who couldn't handle what you could handle? When have you been confused by someone who claimed to be able to do something that you knew would lead to sin if you did it?

> *My rule is simple: If my wife is not part of my friendship with another woman, it's not appropriate for me.*
> — CHUCK

MENANDWOMEN
WWW.MOSAIXSTUDY.COM

## BIG IDEA TWO

Paul also warns the Corinthians not to be too cocky in thinking themselves strong. They might not be as strong as they think they are. Idolatry is a real possibility when one attends parties where idol-meat is served. Likewise, we shouldn't be too cocky when we set our own boundaries. We might not be able to handle as much freedom in an opposite-sex friendship as we think we can.

How much time do you spend thinking about how your relationships are perceived by others? Why?

What does deference have to do with anything? Why would Paul ask us to be so protective or thoughtful of others?

How are we supposed to unify Paul's two directives in this passage: (1) to look out for others and consider how our actions may affect them, and (2) to embrace our freedom in Christ and move forward with confidence in that freedom? Give an example of how you might meet both of these directives.

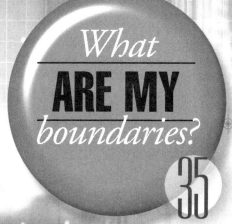

*What ARE MY boundaries?*

> *I was really good friends with a man I went to seminary with. We studied together pretty regularly because we were in the same program. About a year into our friendship his wife told him that she didn't want him to spend time with me anymore—so he ended our friendship. I'm still mad at both of them.*
>
> **—VALERIE**

Paul cares about context. He is quick to say that what may be appropriate in one situation around one group of people may not be in another.

What responsibility do we have to the folks around us? Why do you think Paul asks us to focus on others instead of just ourselves—after all, we're talking about *our* friendships here. What business is it of anyone else?

How much do you care about what other people think, especially as it relates to your relationships?

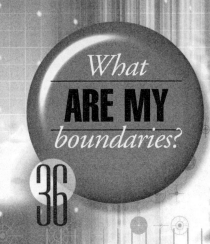

## What ARE MY boundaries? 36

## TWO BIG IDEA

**A DEFERENCE CAVEAT** Let's address two specific groups as it relates to showing deference. The first group is spouses or partners, and the second is our community. The spouse/partner group really needs no definition other than to say that "partner" is someone you are actively dating.

For the sake of clarity, let's define community as the group of people with whom you are closest, perhaps in your Bible study or discipleship group—maybe the folks with whom you are working on this study. It is safe to say that both of these groups should receive special deference.

In what ways, if any, should our spouse, partner, or community receive deference when it comes to our opposite-sex relationships?

Do you think the people who represent these groups in your life feel the freedom to express honestly how they feel about your opposite-sex relationships? What would giving them permission in this area involve?

MENANDWOMEN

# BIG IDEA TWO

## AS A GROUP—OR ON YOUR OWN

Boundaries come down to an issue of responsibility. We're each responsible for certain things in our lives—we can't place blame or assume someone else will take responsibility for us. Setting boundaries can be an involved process requiring time, thought, and consideration for others.

Setting boundaries takes a good deal of thought and reflection. Go back to page 26 and look at the list of boundary examples. Are there any boundaries that you need to set within your opposite-sex friendships? What would those boundaries look like? How could you communicate those boundaries to the people you're in relationship with?

As a group, are there any boundaries you need to set that would affect how you relate to one another?

Are there any questions you still have about the material covered in this chapter? If so, what are they? If you're doing this as a group, how could the other people in the group help you answer them? If you're doing this study on your own, where might you turn for answers?

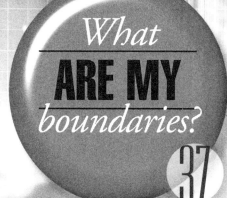

> Your partner must know that your relationship with him or her comes first—before all other friendships. A solid commitment to your own relationship will allow you to have opposite-sex friendships.
>
> —PETER SHERAS, PH.D., PROFESSOR AND CLINICAL PSYCHOLOGIST AT THE UNIVERSITY OF VIRGINIA[5]

## WHAT DOES IT MEAN TO BE SAFE?

In *When Harry Met Sally,* Harry said men and women can't be friends because sex always gets in the way. It's easy to see, then, that there's lots of potential danger in male-female friendships. Without thinking too hard, we could come up with a zillion dangers these relationships could represent.

But given that we find ourselves thrown together in all kinds of situations that have the potential for friendship, the next logical question is to ask how we can be safe for others and ourselves.

*How* **CAN I BE** *a safe person?* 38

> Can't a man say a woman is attractive without it being a come-on?
> 
> **HARRY TO SALLY,**
> **WHEN HARRY MET SALLY**[1]

What do you think it means to be a safe person?

> I've come to the conclusion that, for the most part, men in our culture are not safe for women.... I've been moved to cry to God, "Where are the men to whom women can relate in absolute safety? Where are the men who don't, in their thoughts, body language, preferences, or humor, objectify and degrade women?"
> 
> —**STAN THORNBURG,**
> **"ON BECOMING A SAFE MALE"**[2]

Does that standard apply to everyone, or does it vary from person to person, situation to situation? How do you determine that?

# BIG IDEA THREE

Have you ever been in a relationship with someone of the opposite sex who wasn't safe? How did you know that person wasn't safe? How did that make you feel?

On a scale of 1 to 5, how important is it to you to feel safe in your relationships with the opposite sex?

1      2      3      4      5
not very important      extremely important

> *I try to be honest with my friends in general—whether male or female. I think that makes me a safe person because I try to clearly state my expectations and check back from time to time to make sure those intentions are clear.*
> —SARAH

> *Safe for me is someone who I know isn't going to try to come on to me or take advantage of our friendship. A safe person is usually someone my husband is friends with.*
>
> *I'd like to think that I'm safe. I'm committed to my marriage, so I don't think I'd be a threat to someone else. But sometimes I can come across like I'm flirting—without my even knowing it! I have to be careful about that—especially with my single male friends.*
> —JENNIFER

## How CAN I BE a safe person?

39

## A BIBLICAL VIEW OF SAFETY

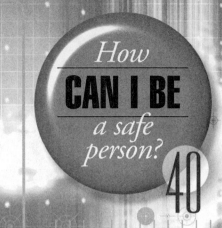

*How* **CAN I BE** *a safe person?* 40

If you've gotten anything at all out of following Christ, if his love has made any difference in your life, if being in a community of the Spirit means anything to you, if you have a heart, if you *care*—then do me a favor: Agree with each other, love each other, be deep-spirited friends. Don't push your way to the front; don't sweet-talk your way to the top. Put yourself aside, and help others get ahead. Don't be obsessed with getting your own advantage. Forget yourselves long enough to lend a helping hand.

Think of yourselves the way Christ Jesus thought of himself. He had equal status with God but didn't think so much of himself that he had to cling to the advantages of that status no matter what. Not at all. When the time came, he set aside the privileges of deity and took on the status of a slave, became *human*! Having become human, he stayed human. It was an incredibly humbling process. He didn't claim special privileges. Instead, he lived a selfless, obedient life and then died a selfless, obedient death—and the worst kind of death at that: a crucifixion.

Because of that obedience, God lifted him high and honored him far beyond anyone or anything, ever, so that all created beings in heaven and on earth—even those long ago dead and buried—will bow in worship before this Jesus Christ, and call out in praise that he is the Master of all, to the glorious honor of God the Father.

What I'm getting at, friends, is that you should simply keep on doing what you've done from the beginning. When I was living among you, you lived in responsive obedience. Now that I'm separated from you, keep it up. Better yet, redouble your efforts. Be energetic in your life of salvation, reverent and sensitive before God. That energy is *God's* energy, an energy deep within you, God himself willing and working at what will give him the most pleasure.

Do everything readily and cheerfully—no bickering, no second-guessing allowed! Go out into the world uncorrupted, a breath of fresh air in this squalid and polluted society. Provide people with a glimpse of good living and of the living God. Carry the light-giving Message into the night so I'll have good cause to be proud of you on the day that Christ returns. You'll be living proof that I didn't go to all this work for nothing. (Philippians 2:1-16)

THREE BIG IDEA

MENANDWOMEN
www.mosaixstudy.com

# BIG IDEA THREE

Take a minute to summarize what Paul is saying here. What do you think Paul's main point is?

What are some of the character traits Paul mentions in this passage? List as many as you can.

For each of the traits you listed, how would that trait create a sense of safety for the opposite sex?

Are there any particular traits that would add to the safety of your group? Your work environment?

How might you use those traits to determine whether someone is safe? Whether you are safe for others? Think of some questions that might help you evaluate someone else's safety or your own.

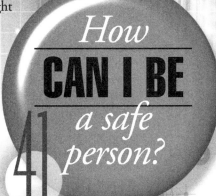

How CAN I BE a safe person?

> Jesus set an example of purity and integrity in His relationships with women. They felt free to approach Him without fear or intimidation. Their best interests were always His top priority. Christ not only refused to treat women as inferiors, He sought to empower them and encourage them in positive, tangible ways.
>
> —STAN THORNBURG, "ON BECOMING A SAFE MALE"[3]

# How CAN I BE a safe person?

42

## THREE BIG IDEA

### NO FEAR

Read the above quote from Stan Thornburg. How do you see Jesus setting this example in his encounter with the Samaritan woman in John 4:1-26? How did he demonstrate each of these things? How did the Samaritan woman respond?

> Safe people are individuals who draw us closer to being the people God intended us to be. Though not perfect, they are "good enough" in their own character that the net effect of their presence in our lives is positive. They are accepting, honest, and present, and they help us bear good fruit in our lives.
>
> —DR. HENRY CLOUD AND DR. JOHN TOWNSEND, *SAFE PEOPLE*[4]

**DO** Read through the Gospels and look for times when Jesus encountered women—Mary and Martha, the woman who touched his hem to be healed, his mother, Mary Magdalene, and others. How would you characterize his interaction with women? What would you say was his policy for relationships with women?

MENANDWOMEN
WWW.MOSAIXSTUDY.COM

# BIG IDEA THREE

**LET'S PLAY "WHAT IF?"** Go back to the Scripture passages you read in the previous section. Keeping them in mind, think about the following scenarios. How does what you read in Scripture affect your responses?

- You really want to be friends with a person of the opposite sex at your office. You've seen this person at your church a couple of times, and from what you know you think you two would really hit it off—and after all, you work at the same place and everyone could use a friend at work who shares similar beliefs. You are already romantically involved with someone else, so you figure there's very little risk of sending the wrong signals as you approach this person. How do you convey that you are a "safe" person? How do you determine if that person is safe too?

> **Safe People:** *How to Find Relationships That Are Good For You and Avoid Those That Aren't* (Zondervan) by Dr. Henry Cloud and Dr. John Townsend is a great book on this topic. Especially helpful is the way they identify traits of unsafe people.

- In the past you had a bit of a reputation as a party animal—you used to go out drinking, and more than once you ended up with someone you shouldn't have in a way that you now regret. When you run into people you used to hang out with, you're uncomfortable because you know how different you are today and you don't want them to think of you as your old self. One Saturday you are in the Christian bookstore shopping for CDs. One of the old gang comes in. You're shocked! *This person can't be a Christian!* you think to yourself. You try to duck behind a display, but it's too late; you've been spotted. So you walk up to each other and begin to chat. What do you say? How do you let this person know who you are now? How do you find out who he or she is now?

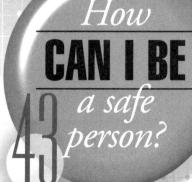

How **CAN I BE** *a safe person?*
43

> Just be smart about what you do together, and know that you don't have to follow your impulses. Not every male/female connection has to be sexual. It is very possible for a man and a woman to have a fulfilling long-term relationship that remains strictly platonic.
>
> —PETER SHERAS, PH.D., PROFESSOR AND CLINICAL PSYCHOLOGIST AT THE UNIVERSITY OF VIRGINIA[5]

## NO FEAR (cont'd)

- You have established a rule for yourself that you won't be alone with a person of the opposite sex in anything other than a very public place. One night after church a person of the opposite sex, whom you would consider an acquaintance at best, asks you for a ride home. You are there by yourself, and this person's house is right on your way home. You don't have any reason other than your rule not to comply. What do you do? If you're the person on the other side of the equation, how do you respond?

*How* **CAN I BE** *a safe person?* 44

- A very close friend of the opposite sex comes to town for a visit. You have been friends forever. Your friend doesn't have much money, and in the days leading up to the visit, it becomes apparent that he or she expects to stay with you. As far as you know, there are no romantic interests or intentions in play. What do you do? What factors might you take into consideration in making this decision?

- You have a tendency to objectify the opposite sex. It's nothing outrageous: you whistle as a particularly attractive person passes; you make eye contact during a conversation, then quickly and carefully cast your eyes... elsewhere. Inside, you know that's not who you want to be. You want to be safe and trustworthy, and you're afraid that someday you're going to be called on the carpet. Can you change? What's it going to take?

> *Being safe means being able to withstand the close scrutiny of my wife or a leader in my church.*
> —CHUCK

THREE BIG IDEA

MENANDWOMEN
www.mosaixstudy.com

## BIG IDEA THREE

## SOME THOUGHTS ABOUT SAFETY

*I try to act in a way that is above reproach. With my married male friends, I don't ever want there to be a question from their wives about my motives. I think, "If I were married, would I let my husband have a friendship with someone like me in this way?"*

—LISA

*For men especially, we may sometimes lead a woman to a deep level of intimacy without ever intending to pursue a romantic relationship that could lead to marriage. As men, we have a tremendous responsibility to be intentional, to communicate, and to address any ambiguity in the context of the friendship. Though it may feel great to connect with a woman, if it's implicitly promising more than you intend, back off.*

—ADAM

*I tend to be an affectionate person. When I see women at church I know I will often give them a hug or make some sort of physical contact. But I think maybe sometimes I send the wrong signal. I really don't mean anything by those gestures, but I'm not sure these women know that.*

—BRANDON

*I'm in at least one relationship where I won't be alone with this particular guy. He creeps me out because he's made it clear that he wants to be more than friends. I don't. Every time we're together he acts hurt and like I've done this terrible thing to him. We used to be friends, but I wouldn't consider us to be friends anymore.*

—DONNA

*How* **CAN I BE** *a safe person?*

45

## PRINCIPLES FOR SAFETY[6]

A safe person:

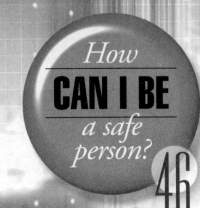

*How* **CAN I BE** *a safe person?* 46

- Assigns worth to others based on absolute rather than relative value. This means that a safe person sees others primarily as children of God rather than blondes, brunettes, and redheads or jocks, nerds, and geeks.

- Keeps his or her own ego in check. This means that a safe person accepts compliments and criticism as easily from one sex as the other.

**THREE**

**BIG IDEA**

- Takes responsibility for his or her own sexual response. This means that a safe person doesn't excuse sexual feelings by blaming it on how another person looks, dresses, or acts.

- Listens to understand the other person's perspective. This means that a safe person realizes that those of the opposite sex are different and seeks to understand what that person is really saying.

- Works to separate emotional intimacy from sexual intimacy. This means that a safe person understands that our culture's insistence that emotional intimacy must be expressed sexually is just plain wrong.

- Has already made up his or her mind about personal sexual ethics. This means that a safe person loves others in a way that it would be unthinkable to consider adultery or fornication.

- Refuses to stereotype the opposite sex. This means that a safe person views each person as an individual and realizes that what may be safe for one person may be uncomfortable or threatening to another.

MENANDWOMEN
www.mosaixstudy.com

# BIG IDEA THREE

> Stereotyping (magnifying the differences between the sexes) is harmful and negative, both to women and men. Stereotyping causes us to judge or reject others without getting to know them... and to limit our own or another's response to God's calling.
>
> —**KAYE COOK AND LANCE LEE,**
> *MAN AND WOMAN: ALONE AND TOGETHER*[7]

- Works to encourage safe and appropriate boundaries for others who have difficulty setting their own boundaries. This means that a safe person acknowledges the need for boundaries and encourages and affirms those boundaries in others.

In conclusion: A safe person does not pressure anyone to behave in a way that makes that person uncomfortable in order to feel loved or appreciated. A safe person does not encourage others to move to a new level of intimacy based on defrauding that person about his or her commitment. A safe person does not compare, discuss, or address another person in a way that indicates value is primarily in appearance or sexual availability.

As you read through the list above, are there any characteristics of a safe person that you lack? How can you work to develop those characteristics? Do you know anyone who exhibits that characteristic who could offer you some insight or guidance in its development?

*How* **CAN I BE** *a safe person?* 47

**LET'S PLAY "WHAT IF?"** As you read the following scenarios, think about the principles for safety on the previous pages and how you would apply them to these situations.

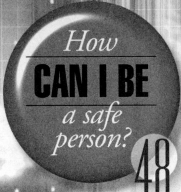

- You're a single guy at a party. One of your female friends has had one too many glasses of wine at dinner, and she catches you out on the deck by yourself. She makes it clear that if you're interested, she is willing to become "more than friends" right there and then. What do you say? And what do you say when you see her next week at church?

- You're a single woman. You're with one of your male friends after singles group. He has been going through a difficult time, so you take time to talk and pray with him. He is pouring his heart out to you, and maybe you're feeling a little uncomfortable, but you figure that he really needs a friend right now. After about forty-five minutes you decide it's time to get out of there. You give him a hug goodbye, but he doesn't let go, and he still doesn't let go, and he *still* doesn't let go. What do you do?

- You are one of very few attractive, single women at your office. Your office is heavily populated by young, relatively good-looking single guys. You want to be considered part of the team, but every guy in the place keeps hitting on you. You don't doubt that their motives are pure—after all, you are certainly date-worthy. But you've been warned that dating guys from the office can lead to problems. How do you handle these guys without messing up the environment you work in?

BIG IDEA THREE

MENANDWOMEN
WWW.MOSAIXSTUDY.COM

# BIG IDEA THREE

You are male and have been volunteering with the youth group at your church for about six months. You are working toward a degree in youth ministry at the local Christian college, so this experience is valuable. One of the girls in the youth group hangs around you a lot, sitting where you sit, going where you go, and so on. Lately she has been baking you cookies and sending you notes. She isn't at all sexually forward with you, but you have a sinking feeling there may be a crush involved. You know from your time around the group that her dad left a couple of years ago and that she hardly ever gets to see him. You don't want to deepen her mistrust of men. What do you do?

## AS A GROUP—OR ON YOUR OWN

Because there is potential danger in male-female relationships—especially concerning sex—it's important not to go blindly forth in those friendships. We must be concerned with safety—for ourselves and for others—if those relationships are to provide us with an opportunity to reflect God's nature as a friend.

What is the most important thing you realized from this discussion on safety? Why was that critical for you?

If you're doing this study as a group, spend some time affirming each other for being safe. How do you see people in the group demonstrating safety? How has their safety affected your experience of the group?

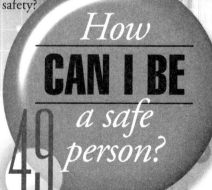

*How* **CAN I BE** *a safe person?*

49

Are you currently in any relationships where you don't feel safe? How might setting boundaries (from the previous chapter) help?

## SO WHAT'S A MOTIVE?

According to the dictionary, a motive is "an impulse that causes one to act in a particular manner; causing or able to cause motion."[1]

Think about the friendships you have. What motivates you to be in those relationships?

> He makes me feel really good about myself.
> Her life is messed up, and she needs me right now.
> He seems lonely, and I want to reach out because it seems that no one else will.

**50 What ARE my motives?**

*Motive is the intention of the relationship or what you're seeking from it. What is the payoff you're seeking? That should be the first maintenance question of all relationships, starting with God and working down. Are we out for ourselves alone or are we putting the other person before ourselves?*

— GLENN

> She always pays for things when we go out as a group.
> He's really popular/smart/attractive, and I think some of it will rub off on me.
> She's part of a crowd that I want to be part of.
> He and I both enjoy doing the same things.
> She's totally hot looking, and I enjoy checking her out.
> He's really confident and makes me feel more confident too.
> She's a CPA and can probably help me do my taxes.
> He's a lot like my brother, and being around him makes me less homesick.
> She's a new believer who is really open to studying the Bible right now.
> He's my boss and, if we're friends, maybe I'll get promoted.

**BIG IDEA FOUR**

MENANDWOMEN
www.mosaixstudy.com

# BIG IDEA FOUR

Are your motivations to be in same-sex friendships different from those in your opposite-sex friendships? If so, how? If not, why do you think that is?

> A man's most open actions have a secret side to them.
> —JOSEPH CONRAD[2]

What role do motives play in your friendships? Have you ever thought or talked about your motives?

The Galatian church struggled with motive. They had tasted freedom in Christ, but instead of using that freedom to live the way God wanted, they became wrapped up in legalism—obeying rules that interfered with loving God and others. They compared themselves with others and constantly worried about their status among others.

Paul wanted them to look at *why* they were doing what they were doing. Was it out of love for God and one another, or was it to make themselves look and feel better?

It is absolutely clear that God has called you to a free life. Just make sure that you don't use this freedom as an excuse to do whatever you want to do and destroy your freedom. Rather, use your freedom to serve one another in love; that's how freedom grows. For everything we know about God's Word is summed up in a single sentence: Love others as you love yourself. That's an act of true freedom. If you bite and ravage each other, watch out—in no time at all you will be annihilating each other, and where will your precious freedom be then?

## 51 — *What* ARE *my motives?*

## 52 — What ARE my motives?

My counsel is this: Live freely, animated and motivated by God's Spirit. Then you won't feed the compulsions of selfishness. For there is a root of sinful self-interest in us that is at odds with a free spirit, just as the free spirit is incompatible with selfishness. These two ways of life are antithetical, so that you cannot live at times one way and at times another way according to how you feel on any given day. Why don't you choose to be led by the Spirit and so escape the erratic compulsions of a law-dominated existence?

It is obvious what kind of life develops out of trying to get your own way all the time: repetitive, loveless, cheap sex; a stinking accumulation of mental and emotional garbage; frenzied and joyless grabs for happiness; trinket gods; magic-show religion; paranoid loneliness; cutthroat competition; all-consuming-yet-never-satisfied wants; a brutal temper; an impotence to love or be loved; divided homes and divided lives; small-minded and lopsided pursuits; the vicious habit of depersonalizing everyone into a rival; uncontrolled and uncontrollable addictions; ugly parodies of community. I could go on.

> *I think men and women can be friends, but it doesn't always work out the way that you'd think. For whatever reason it doesn't seem like we're honest with one another. There seem to be underlying motives in almost everything that we do— we are always playing an angle. I know that this is a pretty sad view to have, but I've seen it play out this way.*
>
> —JAY

This isn't the first time I have warned you, you know. If you use your freedom this way, you will not inherit God's kingdom.

But what happens when we live God's way? He brings gifts into our lives, much the same way that fruit appears in an orchard— things like affection for others, exuberance about life, serenity. We develop a willingness to stick with things, a sense of compassion in the heart, and a conviction that a basic holiness permeates things and people. We find ourselves involved in loyal commitments, not needing to force our way in life, able to marshal and direct our energies wisely.

**FOUR BIG IDEA**

MENANDWOMEN
WWW.MOSAIXSTUDY.COM

# BIG IDEA FOUR

Legalism is helpless in bringing this about; it only gets in the way. Among those who belong to Christ, everything connected with getting our own way and mindlessly responding to what everyone else calls necessities is killed off for good—crucified.

Since this is the kind of life we have chosen, the life of the Spirit, let us make sure that we do not just hold it as an idea in our heads or a sentiment in our hearts, but work out its implications in every detail of our lives. That means we will not compare ourselves with each other as if one of us were better and another worse. We have far more interesting things to do with our lives. Each of us is an original. (Galatians 5:13-26)

How would you summarize what Paul is saying here in a few sentences?

**DO** *Can you think of a movie that depicts good or bad motives having good or bad effects on a relationship? Rent the movie, bring it to your group, and play about ten minutes of the video to show those motives in action.*

According to Paul, what are some good motives for relationship?

What bad motives does he mention?

## 53 What ARE my motives?

Look at Paul's list of things that result from selfish motives. How might these things play out in opposite-sex friendships? Have you ever seen this happen? What was the result?

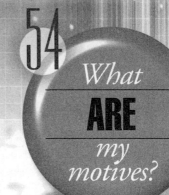

## 54
## *What* **ARE** *my motives?*

> For women, friendships with men often provide the warmth of a big-brother feeling and a chance to joke around. For men, opposite-sex friendships often provide an emotional intimacy that may be missing in their same-sex friendships.
> 
> —**LINDA SAPADIN, PH.D.**[3]

# FOUR

## BIG IDEA

**DO** — What does a motive look like? Draw or paint a picture that depicts what a motive is. Share your creation with the group and explain how you came up with it. Why did you choose the colors you did? The shapes you did?

If we were peeling an onion, motive might be the layer right under safety. As we learned in the last chapter, safety has a lot to do with behaviors and attitudes. Motive has more to do with what's going on deeper inside—it's what causes us to act in a particular manner. It is the stuff down below the surface that comes out in what we say, and how we act, think, and feel.

In the context of this discussion, motive has everything to do with *why*—why we want to be friends with someone, what we hope to get out of it, what needs we are looking to have met, and in some cases, what we secretly want but would never be willing to say out loud, or even admit to ourselves.

# BIG IDEA FOUR

**WHAT'S THE BIG DEAL?** "As long as I do the right thing, what does it matter what my motives are?" Seems like a reasonable question.

Jesus has something to say about all this. In Matthew 5, he makes it clear that he's just as concerned about what goes on in our heads and hearts as what comes out in how we behave.

> "You're familiar with the command to the ancients, 'Do not murder.' I'm telling you that anyone who is so much as angry with a brother or sister is guilty of murder. Carelessly call a brother 'idiot!' and you just might find yourself hauled into court. Thoughtlessly yell 'stupid!' at a sister and you are on the brink of hellfire. The simple moral fact is that words kill . . .
>
> "You know the next commandment pretty well, too: 'Don't go to bed with another's spouse.' But don't think you've preserved your virtue simply by staying out of bed. Your *heart* can be corrupted by lust even quicker than your *body*. Those leering looks you think nobody notices—they also corrupt. (Matthew 5:21-22,27-28)

What's Jesus' opinion of the importance of motives?

> We are all selfish and I no more trust myself than others with a good motive.
> —LORD BYRON[4]

What ARE my motives?

## 56 What ARE my motives?

How does reading this passage make you feel?

We all have thoughts that we'd rather not have. How do you deal with those "stupid" thoughts and "leering looks"?

Why do you think Jesus took the law to a deeper level? What point do you think he was trying to make here?

**FOUR BIG IDEA**

> *I am terrible at determining appropriateness with my male friends. I'm talking about emotional appropriateness. Physical appropriateness is a different thing altogether. I think you have to draw the line when your intentions start to bleed over the line into wishing that you had a different kind of relationship.*
>
> —SARAH

MENANDWOMEN
www.mosaixstudy.com

# BIG IDEA FOUR

It's clear that it isn't just what we do (murder, adultery, and so on) but what we think (anger, lust, or envy) that matters. So this section will give us an opportunity to look below the surface and make sure not only that we are *doing* the rights things, but that our motivations are in the right place as well.

> Sometimes I think that guys assume they've cornered the market on lust. I know how I feel when some hot guy walks in our group. It's not like I'm going to go jump on him, but I might think about it a little [laughing].
>
> —SHELLEY

The challenge is this: Our external behaviors are apparent to those around us, so most of us work hard to make sure they are appropriate. But the stuff that goes on inside our heads is hidden, so it's harder to make sure that stuff is appropriate.

Often we are in relationships where we are accountable for our behavior. What would you think about being in a same-sex relationship where you were committed to be accountable for your thought life too? Have you ever been a part of something like that? What was the result?

## 57 What ARE my motives?

> My wife and I have a mutual friend. Actually she's more my wife's friend, but I found myself trying to spend time around her when she's over at the house. I admitted to my wife that I was attracted to her, but she said that we're always going to be attracted to other people—it's what we do with it that matters. She didn't really seem that mad about it and I thought I was making this big confession. But now I feel like I have permission to be attracted to other people, and that doesn't seem right either.
>
> —DANIEL

If you feel comfortable doing so, tell the group about a time when what you were doing on the outside was radically different from what you were thinking on the inside. How did you resolve the difference between your actions and your attitudes? What, if anything, would you do differently if faced with a similar situation in the future?

## 58 What ARE my motives?

> We should often be ashamed of our finest actions if the world understood all the motives behind them.
>
> —FRANÇOIS, DUC DE LA ROCHEFOUCAULD[5]

**ASKING THE HARD QUESTIONS** Being honest with ourselves is the key to making sure our motives are good and our hearts are in the right place. One person we interviewed responded in this way:

*When examining my motives, I ask myself a lot of questions. I've looked at my emotional reactions in different situations. Sometimes my initial emotional response (be it anger, sadness, or jealousy) can tell me more than logic can. Basically I ask myself three groups of questions:*

1. *Am I physically attracted to this person? If so, is it too much for me to control myself or make respectful decisions?*
2. *What do I want from this friendship? Am I looking for a spouse in this person? Am I looking for an intimate friendship? Am I just looking for someone to have fun with?*
3. *Do I have the absolute best for this person at heart? Are my desires biblical? Are they helping or hurting other relationships this person has?*

—LISA

FOUR BIG IDEA

MENANDWOMEN
www.mosaixstudy.com

## BIG IDEA FOUR

Lisa's questions may not be the right ones for you. Come up with a list of questions that you might ask yourself to get to the heart of what your real motives are for a relationship. If you feel comfortable, share your questions with the group.

> *What are my true intentions? What is my goal in pursuing a particular action? If I can answer those questions, I can define my motive.*
> —MEGAN

> *I think the most important questions to ask myself are these: "Why am I pursuing intimacy with this woman?" and "What level of intimacy is appropriate for this relationship?"*
> —ADAM

59 — What ARE my motives?

**WHAT ARE YOUR INTENTIONS?** As I've watched my male friends, one of the patterns I've noticed is the desire to enjoy deep emotional intimacy with a woman without ever "officially" telling her that he wants to pursue a romantic relationship with her. He calls it "friendship," yet he's initiating emotional intimacy on such a deep level that it invites the woman to share her heart and, over time, to hope for much more.

When she eventually calls him on it and he says that he just wants to be "friends," she's deeply hurt and confused by the inconsistency between his words and his actions. He says "friendship," but the depth of intimacy he wants to enjoy with her communicates a desire for more.

60

What ARE my motives?

More than once I've heard guys rant about how they don't understand why she has to be so demanding, or how she ever got the idea that he was going to offer her more than was clearly on the table. Yet men often seem unable to see how the kind of relationship they've defined in reality was more than "friendly" all the way along.

This can certainly happen the other way around. It behooves all of us to pay attention to what's happening in our relationships with members of the opposite sex. If we're initiating one-on-one time with them, what are we pursuing? Why do you want to go deeper? Are you willing to think about the possibility of something deeper and be up front about it? Or do you simply want to enjoy the benefits of intimacy without the associated risk?

Though we might not immediately recognize it as such, this approach to relationships and intimacy is really no different than having casual sex with people without the commitment. We want to enjoy the tender comforts of being close to someone without making a commitment to a long-term relationship, or without at least committing to exploring the potential of marriage to that person.

When we do that, we run the risk of hurting others or being hurt badly ourselves because we're not willing to be real enough, to care enough to state our intentions up front.

—ADAM

FOUR BIG IDEA

MENANDWOMEN
www.mosaixstudy.com

## BIG IDEA FOUR

### AS A GROUP—OR ON YOUR OWN

Most of us know that what goes on in our head and heart is eventually going to come out of our mouth or in our actions (even if we really hope it won't). Getting in touch with and evaluating our motives—and conforming them to God's will for us—will lead to healthier, fuller, and more rewarding relationships with people of the opposite sex.

What is the most important thing you realized from this discussion on motive? Why was that critical for you? What are a few specific things that you think you will do in response?

As a group, how do you think your individual motives are expressed through your interaction with the group? Talk about some of your motives for your involvement with the group. Do you think your motives all have to be the same or at least similar for the group to succeed?

Make a list specific to your opposite-sex friendships of the things you would like to "meditate" on. Or stated another way, what would you like your motives to be? How different are those ideal motives from your actual motives? How can you get from where you are to where you would like to be?

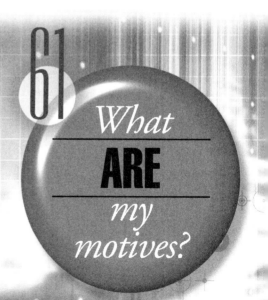

61

*What* **ARE** *my motives?*

## IT'S A COED TEAM

Think about different teams or groups you've been part of. What are some of the advantages and disadvantages to a same-sex team? A coed team?

How **IMPORTANT** are gender differences?

62

> When Christ formed the team we call the Body of Christ, He didn't give us the choice of being on a same-sex team. He decided that we would be more effective if the team was made up of men and women working together toward a common goal.
>
> —R. RUTH BARTON, "WOMEN AND MEN WORKING TOGETHER"[1]

In the quote above, Ruth Barton mentions working toward a common goal. How important do you think it is for men and women to have a common goal or interest in order to work effectively together? What's the value of a common goal?

**DO** There are two mistakes we can make in dealing with the differences between men and women: we can make too little of them or too much of them. The fact is, men and women are alike in many ways and different in many ways. For balance, grab a big sheet of paper and brainstorm all the ways that men and women are alike.

Think about your friendships and work relationships with the opposite sex. Would you say you have a common goal? If so, what is it? If not, what are your different goals?

FIVE BIG IDEA

MENANDWOMEN

# BIG IDEA FIVE

> The combination of the male perspective and the female perspective, working together in partnership, is invaluable in life and ministry.
> —VOLLIE SANDERS, "BIBLICAL FEMININITY"[2]

The above quote by Vollie Sanders isn't specific. What specifically have you found that men bring to the table in working together? What specifically do women bring? How do those things work together? Do you think the combination of the two is "invaluable"? Why, or why not?

**Deborah** Tannen's book *You Just Don't Understand* (Ballantine) is a great guide to understanding the differences in how men and women communicate.

**DO YOU SPEAK MY LANGUAGE?** While we're not supposed to read too much into the differences between men and women, the fact remains that men and women are different. One of the key differences between men and women lies in how we communicate.

Learning the language of the opposite sex is vital if we are to work together toward a common goal. And that's what a friendship is, striving toward the common goal of an effective and meaningful relationship.

## How IMPORTANT are gender differences?

*Men can be more linear and women are more process oriented. Appreciate that in your friendships. Men, don't finish my sentences. Women, ask them how they reached their conclusions. Appreciate the diversity!*

—JAN

## How IMPORTANT are gender differences?

In her best-selling book, *You Just Don't Understand*, Deborah Tannen identifies a number of ways men and women communicate differently. Here's a brief look at some of those differences: [3]

- Independence vs. intimacy

  In a man's world, conversations are negotiations in which people try to achieve and maintain the upper hand. Life is a contest, a struggle to preserve independence and avoid failure.

  In a woman's world, conversations are negotiations for closeness in which people try to seek and give confirmation and support, and try to reach consensus. Life is a community, a struggle to preserve intimacy and avoid isolation.

> *Men are logical and analytical. Women are emotional.*
> —KATHY

- Report talk vs. rapport talk

  For most men, talk is primarily a means to preserve independence. This is done by exhibiting knowledge and skill, and by holding center stage through verbal performance such as storytelling, joking, or imparting information.

  For most women, the language of conversation is primarily a language or rapport: a way of establishing connection and negotiating relationships. Emphasis is placed on displaying similarities and matching experiences.

- Contest vs. community

  To many men, conflict is the necessary means by which status is negotiated, so it is to be accepted and may even be sought, embraced, and enjoyed.

  To most women, conflict is a threat to connection, to be avoided at all costs. Therefore disputes are preferably settled without direct confrontation.

FIVE BIG IDEA

MENANDWOMEN
WWW.MOSAIXSTUDY.COM

# BIG IDEA FIVE

Think about these differences in communication. Come up with some examples of when you've seen these differences in action.

To what extent do you agree or disagree with Kathy, Glenn, and Lisa? As you think about your communication style and that of your opposite-sex friends, does what they say hold true? Or are they just stereotyping?

> *Women speak to be listened to and understood—women listen to understand and hear. Men speak to clarify—men listen to give advice and solve problems.*
> —LISA

> *Not to be absolutist, but men communicate facts and do so verbally. They are not big fans of nuance or imagery. Women are much better on these, but will have difficulty bottom-lining anything for you. They are very descriptive, using body and voice to transmit their message. I think the difference enhances the relationships between men and women.*
> —GLENN

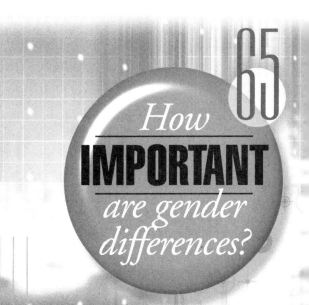

## 65 How IMPORTANT are gender differences?

Have you ever miscommunicated like Dylan? How did you find out that what you said was taken the wrong way? Do you ever change your tone or the phrasing that you use to avoid miscommunication with the opposite sex?

## How IMPORTANT are gender differences?

*I work in sales, and sometimes in the office we use pretty aggressive language about what we do. I might say, "I totally killed that client" or "I'm going to have that guy for lunch." One of the women I work with thought I was actually a really angry person, like I was really mad at the clients, but I totally wasn't. That's just the way I talk about it.*

—DYLAN

## FIVE BIG IDEA

Get a group of men and women together talking about what they think and how they communicate, and you'll hear a lot of "You can't really be thinking that. Can that be true?" Emmanuel Kant wrote that we interpret everything through the grid of our experience. According to Kant, there is the thing, and then there is the way I view or perceive the thing based on everything that I have experienced in my life up to that point.

Describe a situation in which the differences between male and female communication styles were apparent to you.

MENANDWOMEN
www.mosaixstudy.com

## BIG IDEA FIVE

**WORKING TOGETHER** I manage a department of three guys and thirteen women. When I talk to other guys about my department, sometimes they act like it must be a drag. "That must be like an episode of Melrose Place." But those guys couldn't be more wrong.

These women know about creating environments of grace. If we were an all-male department and we missed a sales goal a couple months in a row, chances are there would be recriminations, accusations, and who knows what else. But the women I work with know how to deal with failure in a way that is encouraging and positive—kind of a "we'll get 'em next month" attitude.

These women seem to instinctively know that relationships are more important than anything else. The top salesperson in my department is a woman, and I think she's good because she values her customers for who they are, not just for what they can do for her. She communicates so well with them and seems to be able to connect in a very real and genuine way. And she also sells them a lot of stuff.

These women aren't concerned with ego and image—if there is a female equivalent for "macho," I don't know what it is. As a result, they're great at affirmation. They love to give cards and send little notes of encouragement. I bet that doesn't happen in many all-male departments.

The other day I was feeling full of myself and said something like, "If I just had ten more of me, we could really get things going around here." On the drive home I realized what a dumb thing that was to say. If there were ten of me, I wouldn't even want to come to work. All in all, if I could manage a department full of guys or stay right where I am, surrounded by these women, I wouldn't leave them for anything. By the way, I apologized the next day for my boastful comment, and these women were only too happy to forgive me.

—TOBEN

**DO** Come up with a common scenario (a meal, a sporting event, a concert) and then role-play the way someone of the opposite sex might describe it. Feel free to go wild with the stereotypes, as it will work to illustrate the difference. Talk about why you described the situation the way you did and what the underlying motivation was.

### How IMPORTANT are gender differences?

67

## How IMPORTANT are gender differences?

**STAYING TOGETHER** Men and women are different—God made us that way. So what does the Bible have to say about those differences when it comes to working together?

> In light of all this, here's what I want you to do. While I'm locked up here, a prisoner for the Master, I want you to get out there and walk—better yet, run!—on the road God called you to travel. I don't want any of you sitting around on your hands. I don't want anyone strolling off, down some path that goes nowhere. And mark that you do this with humility and discipline—not in fits and starts, but steadily, pouring yourselves out for each other in acts of love, alert at noticing differences and quick at mending fences.
>
> You were all called to travel on the same road and in the same direction, so stay together, both outwardly and inwardly. You have one Master, one faith, one baptism, one God and Father of all, who rules over all, works through all, and is present in all. Everything you are and think and do is permeated with Oneness. (Ephesians 4:1-6)

How is noticing differences different from focusing on them? Why do you think Paul wants us to notice our differences?

Paul says we should notice differences and mend fences. What do you think that looks like in male-female relationships?

Think back to the people in your life you listed in the first chapter. How are you traveling on the same road with those people? Do you think you're doing a good job of staying together—or do you think you're strolling off in different directions?

FIVE BIG IDEA

MENANDWOMEN

# BIG IDEA FIVE

What about your discussion group? How are you traveling on the same road? How well do you think you're staying together—both outwardly and inwardly—as a group?

## AS A GROUP—OR ON YOUR OWN

Men and women are different—there's no denying it. But those differences add to the diversity of our relationships and help create a complete body.

As a group, how have you benefited from having members of the opposite sex participate?

What are some practical ways you could value the differences you see between men and women rather than complaining about them?

How could you work to be a better person for someone of the opposite sex to work with?

How *IMPORTANT* *are gender differences?*

## LOVING MUCH, WELL, AND APPROPRIATELY

Now that we've looked at all of these things surrounding men and women, the big question is this: So what? What do we do with it?

Many of us have an easy time listening to a sermon, participating in a Bible study, reading an inspiring book. We get easily excited about what we're learning and think about how great life would be if we did whatever it was we'd learned. But usually we go on to the next sermon, study, or book without putting anything into practice. All in all, that's a big waste of time.

Let's pull everything together that we've learned and come up with some practical and possible things to do about male-female friendships that will change how we live every day.

### 70 WRAPPING IT UP
*so what?*

What's a good response to what we know about men and women?

# WRAP UP

> So this is my prayer: that your love will flourish and that you will not only love much but well. Learn to love appropriately. You need to use your head and test your feelings so that your love is sincere and intelligent, not sentimental gush. Live a lover's life, circumspect and exemplary, a life Jesus will be proud of: bountiful in fruits from the soul, making Jesus Christ attractive to all, getting everyone involved in the glory and praise of God. (Philippians 1:9-11)

How do you test your feelings? Is this something that comes naturally to you, or do you have to work at it?

 Why do you think love (especially in a male-female friendship) must be both sincere *and* intelligent?

What does it mean to be "circumspect and exemplary" when it comes to your friendships with the opposite sex?

## WRAPPING IT UP
*so what?*

# 72 WRAPPING IT UP
*so what?*

**TAKE A MINUTE** For most of us life moves pretty fast. We have lots to do and not much time to do it. But if we are to take Paul seriously and attempt to be "circumspect and exemplary," then we're going to need to take some time to stop and think and then weigh what we discover against what we know to be good and pleasing to God.

cir·cum·spect—heedful of circumstances and potential consequences; prudent.

ex·em·pla·ry—worthy of imitation; commendable: *exemplary behavior.* Serving as a model.[1]

> Investigate my life, O God, find out everything about me; Cross-examine and test me, get a clear picture of what I'm about.
> —KING DAVID, PSALM 139:23

On your own: Set aside some time to be by yourself in a place where your are comfortable and can think. Bring along your journal or something to write on. Before you begin, spend a few minutes meditating on the words of David above.

MENANDWOMEN
www.mosaixstudy.com

# WRAP UP

When you are ready, down the left side of the page write the names of any significant friendships with the opposite sex. On the right side write your motivations, intentions, and hopes for those friendships. Be honest—after all, you're the only one looking at this sheet of paper. You can burn it or shred it after you're done if you'd like. But just for an hour, try to be completely frank with yourself.

In the process of searching yourself, if you find some things that aren't exemplary (and almost all of us will), commit to pray about those things for a period of time. If you think it would be helpful, try confiding in a friend and ask him or her to pray with you.

As a group: After you have completed this activity, get together with your group and talk about your experience. There's no need to go into detail—for most of us the process of admitting something to ourselves is hard enough, let alone admitting it to a group of people. But if you feel safe doing so, talk about how you felt throughout the process and what, in general, you think you've learned. Caution: This is an advanced activity, and if there isn't a well-established environment of safety and grace, it might be best to keep this one to yourself.

## AS A GROUP—OR ON YOUR OWN

Now's the time to really think about how to be intentional in your non-romantic relationships with the opposite sex. You need to think critically about these relationships—to understand your thoughts about them, your motives for participating in them, and what role they play in your life.

What are some things you need to do in order to be a safer person for members of the opposite sex? How might your relationships with the opposite sex change if you were to do these things?

Think about the questions you came up with to evaluate your motives (see page 59).

Think about the coed teams you're involved in. What are some ways you could affirm the work of those of the opposite sex?

If you're doing this study as a group, spend some time affirming the impact those of the opposite sex have had on the group. How did they challenge your thinking, cause you to see things from a different perspective, or add to the group?

## GROUP EVALUATION

As you finish this study guide, it's important for your group to evaluate how your time together went and make some decisions about the future. The following questions may be helpful in that discussion.

As a group, what did we do particularly well?

Is there anything we need to improve?

Do we want to continue meeting together? At the same time? At the same place?

What would we like to study next? Another study guide? A book? Something related to this topic, or something totally different?

When will we meet again?

mosaixstudy.com/menandwomen—
## NOTES

### BIG IDEA #1

1. Nora Ephron, *When Harry Met Sally* (screenplay by Ephron, directed by Rob Reiner, 1989).
2. Friedrich Nietzsche, *Human, All Too Human,* ch. 7, aph. 390 (1878). *The Columbia Dictionary of Quotations* is licensed from Columbia University Press. Copyright © 1993, 1995 by Columbia University Press. All rights reserved.
3. Letter, 1 Dec. 1822 (published in *Byron's Letters and Journals,* vol. 10, ed. by Leslie A. Marchand, 1973–81). *The Columbia Dictionary of Quotations* is licensed from Columbia University Press. Copyright © 1993, 1995 by Columbia University Press. All rights reserved.
4. Mary Hunt, *Fierce Tenderness: A Feminist Theology of Friendship* (1991) as quoted in Gilbert Meilaender, "Men and Women—Can We Be Friends?" *First Things* 34 (June/July 1993), pp. 9-14.
5. Lord Darlington, in *Lady Windermere's Fan,* act 2. *The Columbia Dictionary of Quotations* is licensed from Columbia University Press. Copyright © 1993, 1995 by Columbia University Press. All rights reserved.
6. J. August Strindberg, *The Son of a Servant* (1886; tr. by Claud Field, 1913, p.132.) *The Columbia Dictionary of Quotations* is licensed from Columbia University Press. Copyright © 1993, 1995 by Columbia University Press. All rights reserved.
7. Gilbert Meilaender, "Men and Women—Can We Be Friends?" *First Things* 34 (June/July 1993), pp. 9-14.
8. As quoted in "The Friendship Challenge" by Russell Wild, *Cooking Light*, (March 2001), p. 98.
9. Wild, p. 98.
10. Meilaender.
11. C. S. Lewis, *The Inspirational Writings of C. S. Lewis* (New York: Inspirational Press, 1991), p. 246.
12. Quoted in Diogenes Laertius, *Lives of Eminent Philosophers,* "Aristotle," bk. 5, sct. 20.
13. Meilaender.

### BIG IDEA #2

1. Dr. Henry Cloud and Dr. John Townsend, *Boundaries* (Grand Rapids, Mich.: Zondervan, 1992), p. 33.
2. Matthew Henry, *Matthew Henry's Commentary, Volume 2* (Sovereign Grace Publishers, 1972) p. 1031.
3. Gilbert Meilaender, "Men and Women—Can We Be Friends?" *First Things* 34 (June/July 1993), pp. 9-14.
4. *The American Heritage Dictionary,* 2nd college ed., s.v. "deference."
5. As quoted in "The Friendship Challenge" by Russell Wild, *Cooking Light*, (March 2001), p. 100.

## BIG IDEA #3

1. Nora Ephron, *When Harry Met Sally* (screenplay by Ephron, directed by Rob Reiner, 1989).
2. Stan Thornburg, "On Becoming a Safe Male," *Discipleship Journal* 077 (September/October 1993).
3. Thornburg.
4. Dr. Henry Cloud and Dr. John Townsend, *Safe People* (Zondervan, 1995), p. 11.
5. As quoted in "The Friendship Challenge" by Russell Wild, *Cooking Light* (March 2001), p. 100.
6. Based on "On Becoming a Safe Male" by Stan Thornburg. *Discipleship Journal* Issue 077, (September/October 1993).
7. As quoted in R. Ruth Barton, "Women and Men Working Together," *Discipleship Journal* 077 (September/October 1993).

## BIG IDEA #4

1. *The American Heritage Dictionary,* 2nd college ed., s.v. "motive."
2. Joseph Conrad, Razumov, in *Under Western Eyes,* pt. 1, ch. 2 (1911). *The Columbia Dictionary of Quotations* is licensed from Columbia University Press. Copyright © 1993, 1995 by Columbia University Press. All rights reserved.
3. As quoted in "The Friendship Challenge" by Russell Wild, *Cooking Light* (March 2001), p. 98.
4. Lord Byron, Letter, 28 Sept. 1813 (published in *Byron's Letters and Journals,* vol. 3, ed. by Leslie Marchand, 1974). *The Columbia Dictionary of Quotations* is licensed from Columbia University Press. Copyright © 1993, 1995 by Columbia University Press. All rights reserved.
5. François, Duc de la Rochefoucauld, *Sentences et Maximes Morales,* no. 409 (1678). *The Columbia Dictionary of Quotations* is licensed from Columbia University Press. Copyright © 1993, 1995 by Columbia University Press. All rights reserved.

## BIG IDEA #5

1. R. Ruth Barton, "Women and Men Working Together," *Discipleship Journal* 077 (September/October 1993).
2. Vollie Sanders, "Biblical Femininity," *Discipleship Journal* Issue 077, (September/October 1993).
3. Deborah Tannen, *You Just Don't Understand* (Ballantine, 1990). [These principles were taken from throughout the book.]

## WRAPPING IT UP

1. Excerpted from *The American Heritage® Dictionary of the English Language, Third Edition* © 1996 by Houghton Mifflin Company. Electronic version licensed from INSO Corporation; further reproduction and distribution in accordance with the Copyright Law of the United States. All rights reserved.

mosaixstudy.com/menandwomen—
## AUTHORS

**TOBEN AND JOANNE HEIM** are the authors of *What's Your Story? An Interactive Guide to Building Authentic Relationships* (Pinon Press, 1999) and *Great Expectations: An Interactive Guide to Your First Year of Marriage* (NavPress, 2001). Both Toben and Joanne graduated from Whitworth College in Spokane, Washington, where Toben majored in Communication Studies and Joanne majored in Communication Studies and French. They have been interviewed on numerous radio and television programs. Toben currently works as the sales and trade marketing director for NavPress while Joanne writes and stays at home with their daughters, Audrey and Emma. They live in Monument, Colorado.

# LOOK FOR THESE OTHER THOUGHT-PROVOKING BOOKS FROM THE MOSAIX LINE.

### Great Expectations
Perfect for newlyweds or engaged couples, this discussion-oriented book helps you establish realistic expectations of your first years of marriage.
*Great Expectations* (Toben and Joanne Heim) $10

### How to Stay Christian in College
College students or high school graduates will benefit from this preparatory guidebook for keeping their faith while away from home.
*How to Stay Christian in College* (J. Budziszewski) $10

### Walk This Way
This interactive book presents the beatitudes as the "eight steps" to becoming Jesus' disciple, making it easy for anyone to understand what discipleship really means in daily life.
*Walk This Way* (Tim Woodroof) $14

### What's Your Story?
Designed to encourage people to recount their experiences, feeling, values, and beliefs with others, *What's Your Story?* will get you talking about the things that really matter.
*What's Your Story* (Toben and Joanne Heim) $10

### mosaixstudy.com/community
Discover the skills, attitudes, and behaviors that are essential for experiencing genuine Christian community.
*mosaixstudy.com/community* (Toben and Joanne Heim) $7

Get your copies today at your local bookstore, visit our website at www.navpress.com, or call (800) 366-7788 and ask for offer **#6184** or a FREE catalog of NavPress resources.

Prices subject to change.